YOUR KNOWLEDGE HAS VALUE

- We will publish your bachelor's and master's thesis, essays and papers

- Your own eBook and book - sold worldwide in all relevant shops

- Earn money with each sale

Upload your text at www.GRIN.com and publish for free

Lucy Eschenbach

Aus der Reihe: e-fellows.net schüler-wissen

e-fellows.net (Hrsg.)

Band 44

Britney Spears. Rise and Fall of a Star

GRIN Verlag

Bibliografische Information der Deutschen Nationalbibliothek:

Die Deutsche Bibliothek verzeichnet diese Publikation in der Deutschen National-
bibliografie; detaillierte bibliografische Daten sind im Internet über http://dnb.d-
nb.de/ abrufbar.

Imprint:

Copyright © 2013 GRIN Verlag GmbH
Druck und Bindung: Books on Demand GmbH, Norderstedt Germany
ISBN: 978-3-656-69085-6

This book at GRIN:

http://www.grin.com/en/e-book/275406/britney-spears-rise-and-fall-of-a-star

GRIN - Your knowledge has value

Der GRIN Verlag publiziert seit 1998 wissenschaftliche Arbeiten von Studenten, Hochschullehrern und anderen Akademikern als eBook und gedrucktes Buch. Die Verlagswebsite www.grin.com ist die ideale Plattform zur Veröffentlichung von Hausarbeiten, Abschlussarbeiten, wissenschaftlichen Aufsätzen, Dissertationen und Fachbüchern.

Visit us on the internet:

http://www.grin.com/

http://www.facebook.com/grincom

http://www.twitter.com/grin_com

Inhaltsverzeichnis

1.   Introduction

Britney Spears is and has been one of the most famous pop artists for almost fifteen years. She has been trough a lot since then and has progressed from being a cute, blonde teenager to the 31-year old grown woman with two children she is today.

I have always been interested in her and her story, so I chose this topic. In my paper, I follow her story from her childhood days, trough all the trouble the years of 2007 and 2008 have brought her including a massive mental breakdown, to the new success both in private and professional life she has now.

2.   Britney´s childhood

2.1   Early starts of her career

Britney Jean Spears was born on December 2, 1981[1]. She was the second child of Lynne and James Spears, having a four years older brother. She was a highly expected child, as every other woman in the Spears' Family ever had only given birth to sons.

Britney's love for dancing became very early very clear, when she took her first lessons at age two and was the best attending student[2]. Even at this age she was very ambitious and always wanted to give the best performance[3], her dancing teacher then describes her as a perfectionist[4]. At that time she also developed a desire to sing, at first along to the radio in her mother's car[5] but very soon she started singing the hits from the radio on her own and this was when her mother realized that Britney really could sing. The girl started doing little concerts in the bathroom for her stuffed animals[6] and clearly loved performing on stage when the otherwise shy girl suddenly turned

---

[1] C.f. Heard, Christopher: Britney Spears. Little Girl Lost. Montreal: Transit Publishing, 2010. p. 24
[2] C.f. Spears, Britney and Lynne: Britney Spears' Heart to Heart. First Edition. Munich: Wilhelm Goldmann Verlag, 2000 p. 29
[3] C.f. Ibid, p. 25
[4] C.f. Heard, Christopher: Britney Spears. Little Girl Lost. Montreal: Transit Publishing, 2010. p. 25
[5] C.f. Spears, Britney and Lynne: Britney Spears' Heart to Heart. First Edition. Munich: Wilhelm Goldmann Verlag, 2000 p. 18
[6] Ibid, p. 21

extrovert[7]. At that time, when Britney was about seven and had just won her first talent contest[8], her family had some serious financial struggles[9] but decided for Britney to get all the lessons she needed to possibly succeed[10]. Britney had "always been an athletic little girl" and at age five, she started taking gymnastic lessons[11]. She was quite a big talent and soon won some local competitions[12] but eventually gymnastics didn't make her happy anymore. So her mother, despite her heavy doubts, decided to trust her little girl and to allow her to quit gymnastics and focus on singing and dancing.

2.2   New York

When she first auditioned for *The All New Mickey Mouse Club* in Atlanta, Britney was only eight years old. She wanted very bad to be casted and gave her best, but even though the jury was all excited about her, they were convinced that she was too young. But the casting director found her "stunning, so there was no way [he] was going to give up on her"[13], so he arranged for the Spears Family to make contact with a well-known agent in New York City, Nancy Carson. Lynne Spears phoned her as soon as possible, but as it turned out the Spears' didn't have the money to travel to the Big Apple, so they had to send her a package with tapes of Britney singing a few songs. The agent recognized Britney's talent, as she wasn't "just singing, she was performing"[14], so she suggested for the young girl to come to New York with her mother, who was highly expecting her third child at that time.
Their finances were becoming much of a topic in their life anyway; Jamie wasn't working regular[15] so they were often struggling to pay their bills.
When they finally arrived in New York and made it to Nancy's office, Carson finally insisted for Britney to take part in a very intensive training camp that would require her to move to New York. The family decided that Lynne

---

[7] Ibid, p. 35
[8] Ibid, p. 29
[9] Ibid, p. 25
[10] Ibid, p. 26
[11] Heard, Christopher: Britney Spears. Little Girl Lost. Montreal: Transit Publishing, 2010. p. 26
[12] Ibid, p. 26
[13] Christopher Heard: Britney Spears: Little Girl Lost, p. 37
[14] Ibid., p. 39
[15] Christopher Heard: Britney Spears: Little Girl Lost, p. 41

Spears would move to New York with her daughters, even though Jamie Lynn was just a baby.

At the end of the summer, the Spears women were forced to go back to Louisiana without having had a big success. Nancy promised to look for other auditions Britney could go to, but the financial problems were big[16].

But then Carson told them to come back as she had arranged for Britney to participate in a casting for the musical "Ruthless!". She was made understudy for the main role.[17]

The Spears family decided that it was best for Lynne to move to the Big Apple with Britney and baby Jamie Lynn for the time the show ran. At first Britney had much fun at the show but as time passed and she rarely got to play but had to attend every show, she got bored[18].

At that time she also got to participate in *Star Search*, a major talent show in the early 90s. She got really far into the show but in the end the winner was another boy.

Britney and Lynne decided to drop out of "Ruthless!" so they could be home for Christmas.

2.3   The All New Mickey Mouse Club

Just before Britney was turning twelve, she had her second chance for getting cast for the All New Mickey Mouse Club. The competition was tough, as there were other, nowadays famous, back then already very talented kids in the race. For example, there were such big names as Justin Timberlake, Christina Aguilera and Ryan Gosling[19]. But Britney became a member of the cast and thereby a dream came true for her.[20]

The *Mouseketeers* were like a family. All the actors had apartments near the Disney Studios in Orlando, Florida, where the show was recorded. There were some older kids on the show who had been there for a longer time and were idols for the new members of the cast. The children had to attend classes; Disney was very strict when it came to their academic efforts[21]. The

---

[16] Christopher Heard: Britney Spears: Little Girl Lost, p. 46-47
[17] Britney & Lynne Spears: Heart to Heart, p. 47
[18] Ibid., p. 47
[19] Lynne Spears: Through the Storm, p. 84 et seq.
[20] Lynne and Britney Spears: Heart to heart, p.74
[21] Christopher Heard: Britney Spears: Little girl lost, p. 63 - 65

kids were very close and many of them remained friends, even years after the show was cancelled in 1994[22]

3. Britney's relationships

3.1 Justin Timberlake

Britney's Father had had a drinking problem even before her birth[23] but had been able to control it for a long time. But when Britney was 13 he started drinking again and this time Lynne insisted on seeking help. So she took the whole family to a pastor's whom the rest of the family wasn't very fond of, but who foresaw that "if [Britney] and her daddy don't resolve their issues, [...], she will end up clinging to the first real romance in her life. [...]"[24].

Britney and Justin had known each other since the old Mickey Mouse Club days and Britney even had her first kiss with Justin[25]. Years after the MMC ended, Britney and Justin met again as Britney joined Justin's very successful boy band 'N Sync for their tour in 1998 to promote her debut album "... Baby One More Time". But at first, both of them were in a relationship, although even Britney's boyfriend at that time, Reg Jones reveals that [he] "knew they were either already together or would be together real soon"[26].

She tried to get rid of the teenage-girl image she still had, although she clearly wasn't a teenager anymore. The public made a very big deal about whether Britney was still a virgin or not and she was forced to deny that she had ever had sex by her management[27] although her mother later wrote in her book that Britney lost her virginity at age 14[28].

In 2000, the two young stars announced their relationship in public[29] and got engaged in 2001[30].

[22] Lynne and Britney Spears: Heart to heart, p. 74

[23] Lynne Spears: Through the Storm, p. 23

[24] Ibid., p. 85

[25] http://de.eonline.com/news/459658/britney-spears-reveals-her-first-kiss-was-justin-timberlake-says-jason-trawick-breakup-sucked (Last Access on 11/06/13)

[26] Christopher Heard: Britney Spears: Little Girl Lost, p. 113

[27] Ibid., p. 125 et seq.

[28] http://www.dailymail.co.uk/tvshowbiz/article-1052356/Britney-started-drinking-13-lost-virginity-14-took-drugs-15-says-mother-shocking-new-book.html (Last Access on 11/07/13)

[29] http://news.bbc.co.uk/2/hi/entertainment/1519073.stm (Last Access on 11/07/13)

[30] Christopher Heard: Britney Spears: Little Girl Lost, p. 146

They never got married though. In March 2002 Justin ended the relationship because Britney was cheating on him. To Britney it was just a short break, but for Justin the relationship was definitely over.[31]

The breakup hit Britney very hard. It happened when she was promoting her movie *Crossroads* and therefore had to do lots of PR appearances. As she was canceling shows and often disappointed her fans, it became clear how troubled she was by their separation[32] [33].

Justin was affected by their breakup as well, as it is likely after a three-year's relationship. He processed it by writing the song "Cry Me A River" that appeared on his first solo album and was published as a single. The video to the song showed "Timberlake breaking into his ex-girlfriend's house, filming himself making out with another woman on her bed and watching his ex [-girlfriend] as she [comes] home and [showers]"[34] Then she sees the tape he recorded playing on her television The girl that played his ex-girlfriend was a blonde that looked very similar to Britney[35], so it seems very obvious that the video is about Britney, even though he denied that[36].

3.2 Kevin Federline

Despite her personal troubles, Britney was still very successful, Forbes Magazine declared her "most powerful celebrity in the world"[37]. In September 2002 Britney took a break from her career. In the past few months, not only she and Justin had split up, but also her parents. After the divorce, her mother lived in a big mansion near Kentwood that Britney had built for her and her father joined her brother Bryan in her New York apartment[38].

---

[31] Ibid., p. 150

[32] Christopher Heard: Britney Spears: Little Girl Lost, p. 153-156

[33] http://sixtyminutes.ninemsn.com.au/stories/contributors/259121/britney-revealed (Last Access 11/07/13)

[34] http://www.mtv.com/news/articles/1476973/river-about-britney-justin-but-not.jhtml (Last Access on 11/07/13)

[35] Christopher Heard: Britney Spears: Little Girl Lost, p. 157

[36] http://www.mtv.com/news/articles/1476973/river-about-britney-justin-but-not.jhtml (Last Access on 11/07/13)

[37] http://www.people.com/people/archive/article/0,,20137875,00.html (Last Access on 11/07/13)

[38] Christopher Heard: Britney Spears: Little Girl Lost, p. 153

The crew around Britney became disturbed when there were rumors about drug abuse and as Britney's mental condition seemed to get worse. "She was having mood swings – she'd be the high energy performer one minute and then cry uncontrollably for no apparent reason the next". She was not capable to manage all the fame she had accomplished in just a few years[39].

Another notable incident that caused sensation was Britney's famous kiss with Madonna during their 2003 performance at the MTV Video Music Awards. Britney's image to the public clearly had changed[40]

But as her mother says, "Britney's troubles started around the time she gave birth to her beloved surprise baby, Jayden", but Britney was having trouble before. On January 3rd, 2004, she married an old childhood friend in Las Vegas wile partying. The marriage was annulled shortly after. She was partying a lot then and in her mother's opinion it still was to get over Justin[41].

She did come over him eventually, when she met Kevin Federline, later the same year. After three moths of dating they announced their engagement and got married by October[42 43].

The marriage lasted little more than two years until they got divorced in 2006[44], a time in which Britney took another break from her career to start a family[45] what she did when in September 2005 her first son, Sean Preston Federline, was born[46] and his brother, Jayden James only a year and two days after him[47].

Even taking a break, the paparazzi still followed Britney everywhere, what led to an picture of her driving her car with Sean Preston on her lap in early 2006. The picture was on the news the day after it was taken and with it Britney was said to be a bad mother. The image of Britney being

[39] Ibid., p. 159
[40] http://edition.cnn.com/2003/SHOWBIZ/Music/09/03/britney.spears/ (Last Access on 11/07/13)
[41] Lynne Spears with Lorilee Craker: Trough the Storm, p. 124
[42] http://www.cbsnews.com/stories/2004/09/23/entertainment/main645138.shtml (Last Access on 11/07/13)
[43]http://www.thesmokinggun.com/documents/britney-spears/britney-spearss-faux-wedding (Last Access on 11/07/13)
[44] Ibid.
[45] http://www.mtv.com/news/articles/1492692/britney-taking-break-from-her-career.jhtml (Last Access on 11/07/13)
[46] http://www.people.com/people/article/0,,1039012_1107631,00.html (Last Access on 11/07/13)
[47] Lynne Spears with Lorilee Carker: Through the Storm, p. 126

irresponsible was approved as his worried mother had taken Sean Preston to a hospital a moth later after a small incident just to check if he was all right. After a few other incidents like this, Britney had a breakdown in a café, after having been chased by photographers[48].

In November 2006, Spears filed for divorce because of "irreconcilable differences"[49], the couple got divorced by mid-2007. Britney and Kevin were to share the custody of their children, but Federline wanted full custody because he was worried about the kids. "It's about her partying. It's her partying ways that is forcing Kevin to put his foot down", as a source close to him told E! Online magazine[50]. In October, Kevin got the full custody of the children, with Britney being allowed to see them[51]

4.   Breakdown in 2004

4.1   Shaving her head

When Britney was shaving her head bold on February 18, 2007, it was not just a decision out of clear blue sky. Of course it was rather spontaneous a decision[52], but "[She] had tried to shave her head a couple of times. [...] I told her it wasn't a good idea but she didn't listen", as her then personal assistant Kalie Machado tells[53].

Shaving one's head is a serious sign of mental distress, it is even used in some TV shows to show the troubles a female character is going through[54]. Later, she said, she must have been out of her mind[55], so clearly she was not mentally sane.

---

[48] Christopher Heard: Britney Spears – Little Girl Lost, p. 221-223

[49] http://www.people.com/people/article/0,,1556096,00.html (Last Access on 11/07/13)

[50] http://de.eonline.com/news/55767/britney-kevin-back-to-being-single#thyme_comment (Last Access on 11/07/13)

[51] http://edition.cnn.com/2007/SHOWBIZ/Music/10/01/spears.federline/index.html (Last Access on 11/07/13)

[52] Christopher Heard: Britney Spears: Little Girl Lost, p. 241

[53] Ibid., p. 243

[54] http://www.theatlantic.com/sexes/archive/2013/08/when-a-woman-on-tv-is-in-distress-she-cuts-her-hair-off/278465/ (Last Access on 11/08/13)

[55] http://shine.yahoo.com/shine-beauty/16-reasons-why-women-cut-off-hair-003800781.html (Last Access on 11/08/13)

But it was not exactly a surprise that she had a public breakdown like that. As she had gotten more famous, it also had become clear that she could not control all the fame and the sudden wealth when she would go to a jeweler to look at some very expensive jewelry although she was sitting in a wheelchair and recovering from an injury, when she had just gotten famous in 1998[56]. But of course, she had gotten extremely rich and spending a little of that did not seem to be a mistake.

Although her parents divorced in 2002, Britney did not seem very troubled by that, as she had asked her mother before if she was happy in her marriage.[57] So this, for once, seems not to be a reason for Britney's breakdown.

Another problem Britney seemed to have with her fame was all the attention she got. She could not even leave her house without being chased by the photographers.[58] It is understandable that this was not easy for her to handle; in fact, she wanted them to let her alone[59].

A divorce is always a big thing, even after only two years. Britney had married Kevin to have some stability in her instable life. But Kevin had been doing everything to be a star himself, he even recorded an album and published it, but it was no big success for him[60]. So instead of being someone to trust on, he left her alone and fed of her fame to push his own career.

What certainly triggered Britney's breakdown was the alleged postpartum depression she suffered from after having had her second child. It is not unusual for women to be diagnosed with this a few moths after the birth. It would also not have been unusual for Britney to go out and party in that time, as "in manic states, [women] can engage in risk-taking behavior", as Susan Dowd Stone, a licensed clinical social worker and president of Postpartum Support International says. It is also possible that Britney did not know about this mental disorder[61]. So if she really suffered from a postpartum depression it would explain a lot of her behavior.

In November 2006, Britney was first seen partying with Paris Hilton and Lindsey Lohan, but they soon went on going out together on a regular basis.

---

[56] Christopher Heard: Britney Spears: Little Girl Lost, p. 116
[57] Lynne Spears with Lorilee Craker: Through the Storm, p. 114
[58] Christopher Heard: Britney Spears – Little Girl Lost, p. 221-223
[59] Lynne Spears with Lorilee Craker: Through the Storm, p. 227
[60] Christopher Heard: Britney Spears – Little Girl Lost, p. 225-228
[61] http://de.eonline.com/news/54541/britney-and-postpartum-depression (Last Access on 11/09/13)

Britney was photographed wearing no underwear and, another night, having vomited all over herself. Her personal assistant later told the media, "[Britney] was broken hearted" and that "a lot of people deal with heartbreaks that way".[62]

With the parties came the rumors about her abusing drugs. And they must have been true, because just a day before shaving her head, Britney was forced to go to a rehab resort and so she was a few days afterwards[63]. Of course it is possible for her to have been under the influence of drugs when she shaved her head. Another explanation why she shaved her head could be to conceal her regular use of drugs, as these would have been traceable in her hair.

In January 2007, Britney's aunt Sandra, whom she had been very close to, died of cancer. There was not a single paparazzi at the funeral, so for once the family was been left alone.[64]

So there were many reasons why Britney's mental status was not sane, so no wonder that there had to be a breakdown sooner or later.

4.2   Under conservatorship of her father

At the 2007 MTV Video Music Awards, Britney did a poor job in performing. It could have been her comeback and at first she was really into it. She rehearsed properly and her record label got her a new manager and a new personal assistant but soon she would stop rehearsing. She went partying the night before the performance even though she was told not to. The performance itself was a total disaster; Britney did not move her lips in time to the auto tune and she danced halfhearted. The audience was shocked and of course, the performance was the opposite of a success. Soon afterwards, her new manager and personal assistant resigned, as did her lawyer. Britney was now without professional support for her career.[65]

Britney's parents, despite their divorce, still talked to each other often, especially about their daughter whom both of them didn't have much contact to in that time. "[He seemed] the one friendly fish swimming with

[62]Christopher Heard: Britney Spears – Little Girl Lost, p. 231-232
[63] Ibid., p.
[64] Lynne Spears with Lorilee Craker: Through the Storm, p. 128-133
[65] Christopher Heard: Britney Spears: Little Girl Lost, p. 258-264

[her] in a sea of predators. When one of their children is going through something, we are [...] talking things through".[66] Jamie wanted Britney to be under his temporary conservatorship as his worries about her had gotten deeper in late January and the court ruled so on January 31.[67]

In early January, Britney had been allowed to see her sons under the attendance of a court-official. The visit had been normal, but as the children's bodyguard had brought Sean Preston to her car and wanted to get Jayden James, Britney took the child and locked herself in a bathroom with it and thought Kevin would not let her see her children again. The court-official had to call the police who talked to her through the closed door bur could not get her out. It was her ex-husbands lawyer who finally got her to open the door. Britney then was brought to a hospital where she would have had to stay for seventy-two hours but required to be released after just about twenty-four hours.[68] [69]

After being released, Britney and Adnan Ghalib, a paparazzi who had followed Britney and now had become her boyfriend[70] went first to Palm Springs to spend some days and afterwards to an economically priced hotel in Mexico to spend some days under fictional names.[71] This very upset her "personal assistant" who rather seemed to be involved in all of her life, helping her make decisions about her personal life and her career, Osama "Sam" Lutfi. For the past few months, he had followed her on the foot and seemed only to want the best for Britney and claimed that " [He was] Britney's friend and would never hurt her". Nevertheless, her former personal assistant Kalie Machado accused him to be a stalker.[72] And he seemed to be known for manipulating people, what now seems reasonable, as he lately has been linked to Amanda Bynes, a young actress who seems to have now problems that could be similar to the ones Britney had then.[73]

---

[66] Lynne Spears with Lorilee Craker: Through the Storm, p. 156

[67] Christopher Heard: Britney Spears: Little Girl Lost, p. 284

[68] Ibid., p. 276-277

[69] Lynne Spears with Lorilee Craker: Through the Storm, p. 171

[70] http://www.people.com/people/article/0,,20168997,00.html (Last Access on 11/10/13)

[71] Christopher Heard: Britney Spears: Little Girl Lost, p. 279

[72] http://www.celebitchy.com/9838/sam_lutfi_stalked_britney_before_befriending_her_claims_her_ex_assistant/ (Last Access on 11/10/13)

[73] http://www.thesuperficial.com/sam-lutfi-amanda-bynes-britney-spears-former-manager-07-2013 (Last Access on 11/10/13)

Lynne and Jamie Spears were concerned about the way Lutfi was influencing Britney's life, as they got to know how angry he was about her few days of holiday.[74] He might have been worried about losing influence on Britney.

A few days after the bathroom-locking incident, a court decided that Britney was not longer allowed to see her children. Federline's lawyer told the media that Kevin actually wanted to share the custody with Britney.[75]

On January 28, Britney and Lutfi had a fight in what he had called her a "piece of trash" and told her that she did not deserve to get her children back,[76] that made the singer flee her house. He had been mad at her because he felt she did not focus on him enough. The paparazzi that found her sitting apathetic outside her house first took their pictures, of course, but called her father who called her mother. Jamie and Lynne headed for Britney's mansion, Lynne being in the company of a friend.[77]

When they finally made it to the front door, Britney had already left the property. So it was Lutfi who opened the door and he was not pleased to see Jamie. After a while, Jamie was asked to leave the property by a security guard.[78]

5.   Rising again

With the restraining order, Lutfi was almost out of Britney's life. He tried to appeal against the judgment but was told that the courts had acted appropriately by the attorney general.[79] Britney started to spend time with her parents again who arranged for Britney to get her first ever bodyguard, Big Rob, whom she trusted like none of his followers, back. They also talked to her first manager, Larry Rudolph, to do the job again. He was it who introduced Britney to Jason Trawick[80], an agent, who first worked for her and would eventually become her boyfriend.[81]

---

[74] Christopher Heard: Britney Spears: Little Girl Lost, p. 279

[75] Ibid., p. 280

[76] Lynne Spears with Lorilee Craker: Through the Storm, p. 173

[77] Christopher Heard: Britney Spears: Little Girl Lost, p. 285

[78] Lynne Spears with Lorilee Craker: Through the Storm, p.174-175

[79] Christopher Heard: Little Girl Lost, p. 290

[80] Ibid., p. 288

[81] http://www.dailymail.co.uk/tvshowbiz/article-1192140/Britney-Spears-IS-dating-agent-Jason-Trawick.html (Last Access on 11/10/13)

Although Britney indicated that she was not comfortable with her father controlling her life, it seemed necessary for him to do so, as she was still having mood swings.[82]

In mid-2008, Britney regained the right to see her children, even if Kevin still had full custody of them. The court declared that she would gain more time to see them if her behavior stayed stable.[83]

In September, MTV kindly let her perform at the Video Music Awards. She did well in her performance and even won three awards that night. In December, her sixth studio album was released and turned out to be a big success.[84]

When the singer's comeback tour started, there were of course people who were happy to see how find she was, but also people who were worried like her ex-music manager Johnny Wright who thought that "she was thrown back into the money making machine again. [...] She has 170 people living off her" and in some points he was right, because Britney had been required to publish a new album, followed by a tour.[85]

Being with Jason Trawick was good for Britney. He was settled down and "the first guy Britney has dated since Justin Timberlake that actually has a job", a Los Angeles radio personality said.[86]

They got engaged in 2011 but had broken the engagement in early 2013, because Britney wanted to have more children.[87]

Britney did not want to be under her father's conservatorship anymore, as she expressed in court on January 22, 2010. She did not see any sense in her only being allowed to spend $1,500 a week whereas her father got $4,000 a week of her money. But the judge did not see a reason to end the conservatorship, as Britney's condition clearly had gotten better since it lasted.[88]

In 2012, Britney was confirmed to be a judge on the US casting show "The X Factor"[89] and landed her sixth number-one hit in the US by featuring on

---

[82] Christopher Heard: Little Girl Lost, p. 288

[83] Ibid., p. 289

[84] Ibid., p. 291-293

[85] Ibid., p. 294

[86] Ibid., p. 298

[87] http://www.dailymail.co.uk/tvshowbiz/article-2261110/Britney-Spears-confirms-split-fiance-Jason-Trawick-year-engagement.html (Last Access on 11/10/13)

[88] Christopher Heard: Britney Spears: Little Girl Lost, p. 300

[89] http://de.eonline.com/news/307137/britney-spears-will-get-record-15-million-payday-to-be-x-factor-judge (Last Access on 11/10/13)

will.i.am's song "Scream and Shout". [90] Forbes magazine named her "music's to earning woman of 2012"[91]

Britney is to release her eight studio album "Britney Jean" on December 3, 2013.[92] Starting in late December, she will be seen for two years in the Planet Hollywood Las Vegas with her "Britney: Piece of Me" show.[93]

The now 31-year old singer surely had a turbulent life with some ups and some downs. Having started her career very early and having experienced sudden fame, she fell deep after choosing the false to guide her. But with the help of her family and her friends, she again made it to the top and is now at her very best.

[90] http://www.entertainmentwise.com/news/68479/william-Teases-Britney-Spears-Shakira-Alicia-Keys-Collaborations (Last Access on 11/10/13)

[91] http://abcnews.go.com/blogs/entertainment/2012/12/britney-spears-is-musics-top-earning-woman-of-2012/ (Last Access on 11/10/13)

[92] http://www.huffingtonpost.com/2013/09/17/britney-spears-album-release-date-announced_n_3940428.html (Last Access on 11/10/13)

[93] http://www.idolator.com/7484654/britney-spears-vegas-piece-of-me-planet-hollywood (Last Access on 11/10/12)

6. References

Books

Heard, C.: Britney Spears. Little Girl Lost. Montreal: Transit Publishing Inc., 2010.

Spears, L./Craker L.: Through the Storm. A real story of fame and family in a tabloid world. Nashville: Thomas Nelson, 2008.

Spears, L./Spears, B.: Britney Spears' Heart to Heart. Die sensationelle Erfolgsstory des Megastars – erzählt von Britney & Lynne Spears. First Edition. Munich: Wilhelm Goldmann Verlag, 2000.

Internet

BBC News: Britney's engagement denied. http://news.bbc.co.uk/2/hi/entertainment/1519073.stm. Download: 11.11.13, 00:48 Uhr

Carl Williott: Britney Spears Announces 2-Year 'Piece Of Me' Vegas Residency, December 3 Album Release. http://www.idolator.com/7484654/britney-spears-vegas-piece-of-me-planet-hollywood. Download: 11.11.13, 07:13 Uhr

Casey Quinlan: When a Woman on TV Is in Distress, She Cuts Her Hair Off The Newsroom, Mad Men, and Girls have all included this plot point in recent seasons. Why?. Download: 09.11.13, 01:08 Uhr

CBSNEWS: Britney Does It Again. http://www.cbsnews.com/stories/2004/09/23/entertainment/main645138.shtml. Download: 11.11.13, 06:28 Uhr

Celebitchy: Sam Lutfi stalked Britney before befriending her, claims her ex assistant. http://www.celebitchy.com/9838/sam_lutfi_stalked_britney_before_befriending_her_claims_her_ex_assistant/. Download: 11.11.13, 06:56 Uhr

Corey Moss: 'Cry Me A River' About Britney And Justin, But Not: VMA Lens Recap.
Director Francis Lawrence pushed the parallels as far as he could.
http://www.mtv.com/news/articles/1476973/river-about-britney-justin-but-not.jhtml. Download: 07.11.13, 14:23 Uhr

CNN: Spears will lose custody of children.
http://edition.cnn.com/2007/SHOWBIZ/Music/10/01/spears.federline/index.html. Download: 11.11.13, 06:45 Uhr

CNN: Britney would not kiss another woman besides Madonna.
http://edition.cnn.com/2003/SHOWBIZ/Music/09/03/britney.spears/. Download: 11.11.13, 00:56

Diane Sawyer, Jacqueline Payson: Britney revealed.
http://sixtyminutes.ninemsn.com.au/stories/contributors/259121/britney-revealed. Download: 07.11.13, 13:30 Uhr

Daily Mail: 'Britney started drinking at 13, lost her virginity at 14 and took drugs at 15,' says her mother in shocking new book.
http://www.dailymail.co.uk/tvshowbiz/article-1052356/Britney-started-drinking-13-lost-virginity-14-took-drugs-15-says-mother-shocking-new-book.html. Download: 11.11.13, 00:44 Uhr

Daily Mail: 'He's the best thing that ever happened to her': Britney IS dating agent Jason Trawick. http://www.dailymail.co.uk/tvshowbiz/article-1192140/Britney-Spears-IS-dating-agent-Jason-Trawick.html. Download: 11.11.13, 07:01 Uhr

Daily Mail: 'I'll always adore him': Britney Spears confirms split from fiance Jason Trawick... as it's claimed they parted over her wish for more children.
http://www.dailymail.co.uk/tvshowbiz/article-2261110/Britney-Spears-confirms-split-fiance-Jason-Trawick-year-engagement.html. Download: 11.11.13, 07:03 Uhr

Donson, Zach: Britney Spears Reveals Her First Kiss Was Justin Timberlake, Says Jason Trawick Breakup Sucked.

http://de.eonline.com/news/459658/britney-spears-reveals-her-first-kiss-was-justin-timberlake-says-jason-trawick-breakup-sucked. Download: 06.11.13, 20:20 Uhr

Huffington Post: Britney Spears' Album Release Date Announced As Dec. 3 On 'Good Morning America'. http://www.huffingtonpost.com/2013/09/17/britney-spears-album-release-date-announced_n_3940428.html. Download: 11.11.13, 07:11 Uhr

Jennifer Vineyard: Britney Spears Announces She's Taking A Break From Her Career.
In online post, singer says she hurt her knee for a reason.
http://www.mtv.com/news/articles/1492692/britney-taking-break-from-her-career.jhtml. Donwload: 11.11.13, 06:37 Uhr

Joal Ryan: Britney and Postpartum Depression.
http://de.eonline.com/news/54541/britney-and-postpartum-depression.
Download: 09.11.13, 02:23 Uhr
People: Britney Pap-Happy with Her New Guy.
http://www.people.com/people/article/0,,20168997,00.html. Download: 10.11.13, 19:07 Uhr

Melanie Bromley:
Britney Spears Will Get Record $15 Million Payday to Be X Factor Judge.
http://de.eonline.com/news/307137/britney-spears-will-get-record-15-million-payday-to-be-x-factor-judge. Download: 11.11.13, 07:05 Uhr
Shaun Kitchener: will.i.am Teases Britney Spears, Shakira, Alicia Keys Collaborations.
LMFAO and Nicole Scherzinger also involved.
http://www.entertainmentwise.com/news/68479/william-Teases-Britney-Spears-Shakira-Alicia-Keys-Collaborations. Download: 10.11.13, 23:03 Uhr

Michelle Tauber: Britney's Next Act. Pop's Princess Takes a Breather and Talks About the Big Breakup, Her Parents' Divorce and the Girl She Left Behind.
http://www.people.com/people/archive/article/0,,20137875,00.html.
Download: 07.11.13, 15:28 Uhr

People: Britney Spears Files for Divorce.
http://www.people.com/people/article/0,,1556096,00.html. Download:
07.11.13, 19:43 Uhr

People: Britney Welcomes Home Sean Preston.
http://www.people.com/people/article/0,,1039012_1107631,00.html.
Download: 11.11.13, 06:40 Uhr

People: Britney Pap-Happy with Her New Guy.
http://www.people.com/people/article/0,,20168997,00.html. Download:
10.11.13, 19:07 Uhr

Piper Weiss: 16 Reasosns Why Women Cut Off All Their Hair.
http://shine.yahoo.com/shine-beauty/16-reasons-why-women-cut-off-hair-
003800781.html. Download: 09.11.13, 01:10 Uhr

Sarah Hall: Britney, Kevin Back to Being Single.
http://de.eonline.com/news/55767/britney-kevin-back-to-being-
single#thyme_comment. Download: 07.11.13, 21:50 Uhr

Sheila Marikar: Britney Spears Is Music's Top Earning Woman of 2012.
http://abcnews.go.com/blogs/entertainment/2012/12/britney-spears-is-
musics-top-earning-woman-of-2012/. Download: 11.11.13, 07:08 Uhr

The Smoking Gun: Britney Spears's "Faux" Wedding.
Pop star's doomed marriage started with a staged 2004 ceremony.
http://www.thesmokinggun.com/documents/britney-spears/britney-
spearss-faux-wedding. Download: 11.11.13, 06:35 Uhr

The Superficial: Wait. How The Hell Did Sam Lutfi Get Involved With Amanda
Bynes?. http://www.thesuperficial.com/sam-lutfi-amanda-bynes-britney-
spears-former-manager-07-2013. Download: 11.11.13, 06:58 Uhr